Jana Hauschild

SCANDINAVIAN CHRISTMAS CHARTED DESIGNS

DOVER PUBLICATIONS, INC., NEW YORK

Copyright © 1985 by Jana Hauschild.
All rights reserved under Pan American and International Copyright Conventions.

Published in Canada by General Publishing Company, Ltd., 30 Lesmill Road, Don Mills, Toronto, Ontario.
Published in the United Kingdom by Constable and Company, Ltd., 10 Orange Street, London WC2H 7EG.

Scandinavian Christmas Charted Designs is a new work, first published by Dover Publications, Inc., in 1985.

Manufactured in the United States of America
Dover Publications, Inc., 31 East 2nd Street, Mineola, N.Y. 11501

Library of Congress Cataloging in Publication Data

Lindberg, Jana Hauschild.
  Scandinavian Christmas charted designs.

  (Dover needlework series)
  1. Needlework—Scandinavia—Patterns. 2. Christmas decorations—Scandinavia. I. Title. II. Series.
TT753.L55 1985   746.4   85–6810
ISBN 0-486-24914-X

Preface

In the midst of the cold and colorless winter arrives the year's most festive holiday: Christmas. In that joyful gift-giving season, the most favored presents are those hand-made items that have received your very special care and attention.

Here is a book of charted Scandinavian designs ready to use in all kinds of needlework: cross-stitch, needlepoint, knitting, latch hook and crocheting. To suggest ideas for using the designs, completed projects are shown on the covers. You can make the items as illustrated, or develop your own special creations.

Make a cross-stitch tablecloth for the family feast, a needlepoint stocking for Santa to fill, or heart-trimmed place mats. Consider a tree skirt to wrap around the sparkling evergreen, a latch-hook pillow for the den, an afghan crochet coverlet cross-stitched with gift-bearing elves. Designs for singing angels, golden stars, ringing bells and evergreen garlands are among the dozens of charts included. All can be developed into decorations or gifts for family and friends.

General Directions

Most of these designs were originally created for counted cross-stitch, but they are easily translated into other needlework techniques. Keep in mind that in counted-thread work, the finished piece will not be the same size as the charted design unless you are working on fabric or canvas with the same number of threads per inch as the chart has squares per inch. With knitting and crocheting, the size will vary according to the number of stitches per inch.

COUNTED CROSS-STITCH

MATERIALS

1. **Needles.** A small blunt tapestry needle, No. 24 or No. 26.

2. **Fabric.** Evenweave linen, cotton, wool or synthetic fabrics all work well. The most popular fabrics are aida cloth, linen and hardanger cloth. Cotton aida is most commonly available in 18 threads-per-inch, 14 threads-per-inch and 11 threads-per-inch (14-count is the most popular size). Evenweave linen comes in a variety of threads-per-inch. To work cross-stitch on linen involves a slightly different technique (see page 4). Thirty thread-per-inch linen will result in a stitch about the same size as 14-count aida. Hardanger cloth has 22 threads to the inch and is available in cotton or linen. To determine the size of a cross-stitch design, divide the number of stitches in the design by the thread-count of the fabric. For example: If a design 112 squares wide by 140 squares deep is worked on a 14-count fabric, divide 112 stitches by 14 (= 8), and 140 by 14 (= 10). The design will measure 8" × 10". The same design worked on 22-count fabric measures about 5" × 6½".

3. **Threads and Yarns.** Six-strand embroidery floss, crewel wool, Danish Flower Thread, pearl cotton or metallic threads all work well for cross-stitch. DMC Embroidery Floss has been used to color-code the patterns in this volume; a conversion chart for Royal Mouliné Six-Strand Embroidery Floss from Coats & Clark, and Anchor Embroidery Floss from Susan Bates appears on page 7.

Crewel wool works well on evenweave wool fabric. Danish Flower Thread is a thicker thread with a matte finish, one strand equaling two of embroidery floss.

4. **Embroidery Hoop.** A wooden or plastic 4", 5" or 6" round or oval hoop with a screw-type tension adjuster works best for cross-stitch.

5. **Scissors.** A pair of sharp embroidery scissors is essential to all embroidery.

PREPARING TO WORK

To prevent raveling, either whip-stitch or machine-stitch the outer edges of the fabric.

Locate the exact center of the chart (many of the charts in this book have an arrow at the top and side; follow these arrows to their intersection to locate the chart center). Establish the center of the fabric by folding it in half first vertically, then horizontally. The center stitch of the chart falls where the creases of the fabric meet. Mark the fabric center with a basting thread.

It is best to begin cross-stitch at the top of the design. To establish the top, count the squares up from the center of the chart, and the corresponding number of holes up from the center of the fabric.

Place the fabric tautly in the embroidery hoop, for tension makes it easier to push the needle through the holes without piercing the fibers. While working continue to retighten the fabric as necessary.

When working with multiple strands (such as embroidery floss) always separate (strand) the thread before beginning to stitch. This one small step allows for better coverage of the fabric. When you need more than one thread in the needle, use separate strands and do not double the thread. (For example: If you need four strands, use four separated strands.) Thread has a nap (just as fabrics do) and can be felt to be smoother in one direction than the other. Always work with the nap (the smooth side) pointing down.

For 14-count aida and 30-count linen, work with two strands of six-strand floss. For more texture, use more thread; for a flatter look, use less thread.

EMBROIDERY

To begin, fasten the thread with a waste knot and hold a short length of thread on the underside of the work, anchoring it with the first few stitches (*Diagram 1*). When the thread end is securely in place, clip the knot.

To stitch, push the needle up through a hole in the fabric, cross the thread intersection (or square) on a left-to-right diagonal (*Diagram 2*). Half the stitch is now completed.

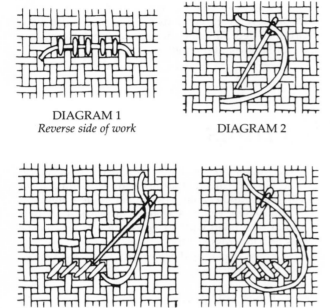

DIAGRAM 1
Reverse side of work

DIAGRAM 2

DIAGRAM 3

DIAGRAM 4

Next, cross back, right to left, forming an X (*Diagram 3*). Work all the same color stitches on one row, then cross back, completing the X's (*Diagram 4*).

Some needleworkers prefer to cross each stitch as they come to it. This method also works, but be sure all of the top stitches are slanted in the same direction. Isolated stitches must be crossed as they are worked. Vertical stitches are crossed as shown in *Diagram 5*.

At the top, work horizontal rows of a single color, left to right. This method allows you to go from an unoccupied space to an occupied space (working from an empty hole to a filled one), making ruffling of the floss less likely. Holes are used more than once, and all stitches "hold hands" unless a space is indicated on the chart. Hold the work upright throughout (do not turn as with many needlepoint stitches).

When carrying the thread from one area to another, run the needle under a few stitches on the wrong side. Do not carry thread across an open expanse of fabric as it will be visible from the front when the project is completed.

To end a color, weave in and out of the underside of the stitches, making a scallop stitch or two for extra security (*Diagram 6*).

When possible, end in the same direction in which you were working, jumping up a row if necessary (*Diagram 7*). This prevents holes caused by stitches being pulled in two directions.

Trim the thread ends closely and do not leave any tails

DIAGRAM 5

DIAGRAM 6
Reverse side of work

or knots as they will show through the fabric when the work is completed.

A number of other counted-thread stitches can be used in cross-stitch. Backstitch (*Diagram 8*) is used for outlines, face details and the like. It is worked from hole to hole, and may be stitched as a vertical, horizontal or diagonal line.

Straight stitch is worked from side to side over several threads (*Diagram 9*) and affords solid coverage.

Lazy daisy stitch and chain stitch (*Diagram 10*) are handy for special effects. Both are worked in the same manner as on regular embroidery.

DIAGRAM 7
Reverse side of work

DIAGRAM 8

DIAGRAM 9

Lazy Daisy Stitch

Chain Stitch

DIAGRAM 10

Embroidery on Linen. Working on linen requires a slightly different technique. While evenweave linen is remarkably regular, there are always a few thick or thin threads. To keep the stitches even, cross-stitch is worked over two threads in each direction (*Diagram 11*).

As you are working over more threads, linen affords a greater variation in stitches. A half-stitch can slant in either direction and is uncrossed. A three-quarters stitch is shown in *Diagram 12*.

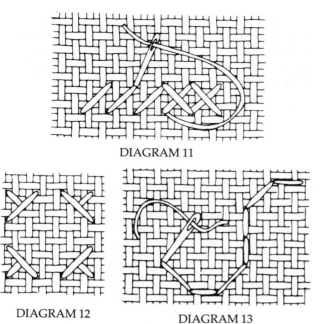

DIAGRAM 11

DIAGRAM 12   DIAGRAM 13

Diagram 13 shows the backstitch worked on linen.

Embroidery on Gingham. Gingham and other checked fabrics can be used for cross-stitch. Using the fabric as a guide, work the stitches from corner to corner of each check.

Embroidery on Uneven-Weave Fabrics. If you wish to work cross-stitch on an uneven-weave fabric, baste a lightweight Penelope needlepoint canvas to the material. The design can then be stitched by working the cross-stitch over the double mesh of the canvas. When working in this manner, take care not to catch the threads of the canvas in the embroidery. After the cross-stitch is completed, remove the basting threads. With tweezers remove first the vertical threads, one strand at a time, of the needlepoint canvas, then the horizontal threads.

FINISHING

Wash the completed cross-stitch in cool water with mild soap. Rinse well, then roll in a towel to remove excess moisture (do not wring). Immediately iron on a well-padded surface, with embroidery right-side down. Allow the piece to dry completely before continuing.

Depending on your project, there are a number of ways to finish the cross-stitch. Tablecloths and place mats can be either hemmed or fringed. To mount a picture, center the work over a white, rag-content mat board. Turn the margins evenly to the back. Working first from top to bottom, lace the margins fairly tautly with sturdy thread. Next, continue to lace the work from side to side in the same manner. (Note: Never use glue for mounting cross-stitch.) Cotton and linen fabrics can be framed under glass; wool needs to breathe and should not be framed under glass unless a breathing space is left.

NEEDLEPOINT

One of the most common methods for working needlepoint is from a charted design. By simply viewing each square of a chart as a stitch on the canvas, the patterns

quickly and easily translate from one technique to another.

MATERIALS

1. **Needles.** A blunt tapestry needle with a rounded tip and an elongated eye. The needle must clear the hole of the canvas without spreading the threads. For No. 10 canvas, a No. 18 needle works best.

2. **Canvas.** There are two distinct types of needlepoint canvas: single-mesh (mono canvas) and double-mesh (Penelope canvas). Single-mesh canvas, the more common of the two, is easier on the eyes as the spaces are slightly larger. Double-mesh canvas has two horizontal and two vertical threads forming each mesh. The latter is a very stable canvas on which the threads stay securely in place as the work progresses. Canvas is available in many sizes, from 5 mesh-per-inch to 18 mesh-per-inch, and even smaller. The number of mesh-per-inch will, of course, determine the dimensions of the finished needlepoint project. A 60-square × 120-square chart will measure 12″ × 24″ on 5 mesh-to-the-inch canvas, 5″ × 10″ on 12 mesh-to-the-inch canvas. The most common canvas size is 10 to the inch.

3. **Yarns.** Persian, crewel and tapestry yarns all work well on needlepoint canvas.

PREPARING TO WORK

Allow 1″ to 1½″ blank canvas all around. Bind the raw edges of the canvas with masking tape or machine-stitched double-fold bias tape.

There are few hard-and-fast rules on where to begin the design. It is best to complete the main motif, then fill the background as the last step.

For any guidelines you wish to draw on the canvas, take care that your marking medium is waterproof. Nonsoluble inks, acrylic paints thinned with water so as not to clog the mesh, and waterproof felt-tip pens all work well. If unsure, experiment on a scrap of canvas.

When working with multiple strands (such as Persian yarn) always separate (strand) the yarn before beginning to stitch. This one small step allows for better coverage of the canvas. When you need more than one piece of yarn in the needle, use separate strands and do not double the yarn. For example: If you need two strands of 3-ply Persian yarn, use two separated strands. Yarn has a nap (just as fabrics do) and can be felt to be smoother in one direction than the other. Always work with the nap (the smooth side) pointing down.

For 5 mesh-to-the-inch canvas, use six strands of 3-ply yarn; for 10 mesh-to-the-inch canvas, use three strands of 3-ply yarn.

STITCHING

Cut yarn lengths 18″ long. Begin needlepoint by holding about 1″ of loose yarn on the wrong side of the work and working the first several stitches over the loose end to secure it. To end a piece of yarn, run it under several completed stitches on the wrong side of the work.

There are hundreds of needlepoint stitch variations, but tent stitch is universally considered to be *the* needlepoint stitch. The most familiar versions of tent stitch are half-cross stitch, continental stitch and basket-weave stitch.

Half-cross stitch *(Diagram 14)* is worked from left to right. The canvas is then turned around and the return row is again stitched from left to right. Holding the needle vertically, bring it to the front of the canvas through the hole that will be the bottom of the first stitch. Keep the stitches loose for minimum distortion and good coverage. Half-cross stitch is best worked on a double-mesh canvas.

Continental stitch *(Diagram 15)* begins in the upper right-hand corner and is worked from right to left. The needle is slanted and always brought out a mesh ahead. The resulting stitch appears as a half-cross stitch on the front and as a slanting stitch on the back. When the row is complete, turn the canvas around to work the return row, continuing to stitch from right to left.

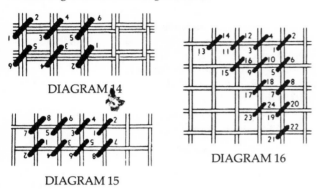

DIAGRAM 14

DIAGRAM 15

DIAGRAM 16

Basket-weave stitch *(Diagram 16)* begins in the upper right-hand corner with four continental stitches (two stitches worked horizontally across the top and two placed directly below the first stitch). Work diagonal rows, the first slanting up and across the canvas from right to left, and the next down and across from left to right. Moving down the canvas from left to right, the needle is in a vertical position; working in the opposite direction, the needle is horizontal. The rows interlock, creating a basket-weave pattern on the wrong side. If the stitch is not done properly, a faint ridge will show where the pattern was interrupted. On basket-weave stitch, always stop working in the middle of a row, rather than at the end, so that you will know in which direction you were working.

FINISHING

When the needlepoint is complete, it must be blocked to give it a professional look. Any hard, flat surface you do not mind marring with nail holes, and will not warp with dampness, can serve as a blocking board. A piece of plywood, an old drawing board, an old-fashioned doily blocker will all work well.

Moisten a terry-cloth towel in cold water and roll the needlepoint in the towel. Leave the needlepoint in the towel overnight to insure that both the canvas and yarn are thoroughly and evenly dampened. Do not saturate the canvas and never hold it under the faucet as that much water is not necessary.

Mark the desired finished size of the needlepoint on the blocking board, taking care that all corners are straight. Stretch the finished canvas on the board, right-side down, and tack the margins with thumbtacks spaced about ½" apart. It may take some pulling to get the needlepoint straight, but do not be afraid of this stress. Leave the canvas on the blocking board, away from direct sun and heat, until thoroughly dry. (Note: Never place an iron on the needlepoint; you cannot successfully block with a steam iron as the canvas must dry in the straightened position.)

KNITTING

Charted designs can be worked into stockinette stitch as you are knitting, or they can be embroidered with duplicate stitch when the knitting is complete. For the former, wind the different colors of yarn on bobbins and work in the same manner as in Fair Isle knitting. A few quick Fair Isle tips: (1) Always bring up the new color yarn from under the dropped color to prevent holes. (2) Carry the color not in use loosely across the wrong side of the work, but not more than three or four stitches without twisting the yarns. If a color is not in use for more than seven or eight stitches, it is usually best to drop that color yarn and rejoin a new bobbin when the color is again needed.

CROCHETING

There are a number of ways in which charts can be used for crochet. Among them are:

SINGLE CROCHET

Single crochet is often seen worked in multiple colors. When changing colors, always pick up the new color for the last yarn-over of the old color. The color not in use can be carried loosely across the back of the work for a few stitches, or you can work the single crochet over the unused color. The latter method makes for a neater appearance on the wrong side, but sometimes the old color peaks through the stitches. This method can also be applied to half-double crochet and double crochet, but keep in mind that the longer stitches will distort the design.

FILET CROCHET

This technique is nearly always worked from charts and uses only one color thread. The result is a solid-color piece with the design filled in and the background left as an open mesh. Care must be taken in selecting the design, as the longer stitch causes distortion.

AFGHAN CROCHET

The most common method here is cross-stitch worked over the afghan stitch. Complete the afghan crochet project. Then, following the chart for color placement, work cross-stitch over the squares of crochet.

OTHER CHARTED METHODS

Latch hook, Assisi embroidery, beading, cross-stitch on needlepoint canvas (a European favorite) and lace net embroidery are among the other needlework methods worked from charts.

SIX STRAND EMBROIDERY COTTON (FLOSS) CONVERSION CHART

KEY: T = Possible Substitute   * = Close Match   — = No Match

DMC NO.	ROYAL MOULINÉ NO.	BATES/ANCHOR NO.
White	1001	2
Ecru	8600	926
208	3335*	110*
209	3415*	105
210	3320*	104
211	3410	108*
221	2570	897*
223	2555	894
224	2545	893
225	2540	892
300	8330	352*
301	8315*	349*
304	2415*	47*
307	6005*	289*
309	2525*	42*
310	1002	403
311	4275T	149*
312	—	147*
315	3130	896*
316	3120	895*
317	1030*	400*
318	1020*	399*
319	5025	246*
320	5015	216*
321	2415	47
322	—	978*
326	2530*	59*
327	3365*	101*
333	—	119
334	4250T	145
335	2525T	42*
336	4270*	149*
340	—	118
341	—	117
347	2425*	13*
349	2400	13
350	2045T	11
351	2015T	11*
352	2015	10*
353	2010*	8*
355	8095	5968
356	8090	5975*
367	5020	216*
368	5005*	240*
369	5005	213*
370	1015	398
371	—	889*
372	—	888*
400	8325*	351
402	8305*	347*
407	8005	882*
413	1025*	401
414	1020*	400*
415	1015	398
420	8720*	375*
422	8710*	373*
433	8265	371*
434	8215	309
435	8210*	369*
436	8205	363*

DMC NO.	ROYAL MOULINÉ NO.	BATES/ANCHOR NO.
437	8200*	362
444	6155*	291
445	6000	288
451	—	399*
452	—	399*
453	1015T	397*
469	5255	267*
470	5255*	267
471	5245	266*
472	5240	264*
498	2425T	20*
500	5125	879*
501	5120*	878
502	5110	876
503	5105	875
504	5100	213*
517	—	169*
518	4860*	168*
519	4855T	167*
520	—	862*
522	—	859*
523	—	859*
524	—	858*
535	1115T	401*
543	8500	933*
550	3380*	102*
552	3370*	101
553	3360	98
554	3355*	96*
561	—	212*
562	—	210*
563	—	208*
564	—	203*
580	5935	267*
581	5925	266*
597	4860*	168*
598	4855*	167*
600	2225*	59*
601	2225*	78*
602	2640*	77*
603	2720*	76*
604	2710	75*
605	2155	50*
606	7260	335
608	7255	333*
610	5825T	889*
611	5735T	898
612	8815*	832
613	5605*	956*
632	8530	936*
640	8625	903
642	8620*	392
644	8800	830
645	1115*	905*
646	1115*	8581
647	1110	8581*
648	1100*	900
666	2405	46
676	6250	891
677	—	886*

DMC NO.	ROYAL MOULINÉ NO.	BATES/ANCHOR NO.
680	6260*	901
699	5375	923*
700	5365*	229
701	5365*	227
702	5330	239
703	5320	238
704	5310*	256*
712	8600*	387*
718	3015*	88
720	—	326
721	—	324*
722	—	323*
725	6215	306*
726	6150*	295
727	6135	293
729	6255	890
730	—	924*
731	—	281*
732	5925T	281*
733	—	280*
734	—	279*
738	8245*	942
739	8240*	885*
740	7045	316
741	6125	304
742	6120	303
743	6210	297
744	6110*	301*
745	6105	300*
746	6100	386*
747	4850	158*
754	8075	778*
758	8080	868
760	2035	9*
761	2030	8*
762	1010*	397
772	—	264*
775	4600*	128*
776	2110*	24*
778	3110	968*
780	8215*	310*
781	8215	309*
782	6230	308
783	6220*	307
791	4165*	941*
792	4155T	940
793	4155	121
794	4145	120*
796	4340	133*
797	4265*	132*
798	4325	131*
799	4250*	130*
800	4310	128
801	8405	357*
806	4870T	169*
807	4860*	168*
809	4145*	130*
813	4610*	160*
814	2340T	44*
815	2530*	43

DMC NO.	ROYAL MOULINÉ NO.	BATES/ANCHOR NO.
816	2530	44*
817	2415T	19
818	2505*	48
819	2000	892*
820	4345	134
822	8605*	387*
823	4400*	150
824	4225	164*
825	4215	162*
826	4210	161*
827	4605	159*
828	4850	158*
829	5825	906
830	5825*	889*
831	5825T	889*
832	5815	907
833	5815*	874*
834	5810*	874
838	8425*	380
839	8560	380*
840	8555	379*
841	8550	378*
842	8505	376*
844	1115T	401*
869	8720*	944*
890	5025*	879*
891	2135	35*
892	2130	28
893	2125*	27
894	2115T	26
895	5430*	246*
898	8425*	360
899	2515	27*
900	7230*	333
902	—	72*
904	5295*	258*
905	5295	258*
906	5285*	256*
907	5280*	255
909	5370	229*
910	5370*	228*
911	5465*	205*
912	5465	205
913	5460*	209
915	3030	89*
917	3020*	89*
918	8330*	341*
919	8095*	341*
920	8060*	339*
921	8060T	349*
922	8315T	324*
924	4830T	851*
926	4820*	779*
927	4810T	849*
928	1010T	900*
930	4510	922*
931	4505	921*
932	4500	920*
934	5070T	862*
935	5225T	862

DMC NO.	ROYAL MOULINÉ NO.	BATES/ANCHOR NO.
936	5260T	269
937	5260	268
938	8430	381
939	4405	127
943	4935*	188*
945	8020*	347*
946	7230*	332*
947	7255*	330*
948	8070	778*
950	8020T	4146
951	8020T	366*
954	5455*	203*
955	5450	206*
956	2170*	40*
957	2160T	40*
958	—	187
959	2515*	186
961	5810*	76*
962	2515	76*
963	2505	49*
964	5150*	185
966	7040	214*
970	7040	316*
971	7045	316*
972	6120*	298
973	6015	290
975	8365	355*
976	8355	308*
977	8350	307*
986	5430	246*
987	5020T	244*
988	5295T	243*
989	5405T	242*
991	5165T	189*
992	4925*	187*
993	4915*	186*
995	4710	410
996	4700	433
3011	5525T	845*
3012	5525*	844*
3013	5515	842*
3021	5430*	382*
3022	—	8581*
3023	—	8581*
3024	1100	900*
3031	—	905*
3032	8620T	903*
3033	8610*	388*
3041	3215*	871
3042	3205*	869
3045	6260T	373*
3046	5810	887*
3047	5805	886*
3051	5530T	846*
3052	5060*	859*
3053	5055*	859*
3064	8005*	914*
3072	4805*	397*
3078	6130	292*
3325	4200	159*

DMC NO.	ROYAL MOULINÉ NO.	BATES/ANCHOR NO.
3326	2115*	25*
3328	2045	11*
3340	—	329
3341	—	328
3345	5025T	268*
3346	5220T	257*
3347	5210*	266*
3348	5270*	265
3350	2220	42*
3354	2210	74*
3362	—	862*
3363	—	861*
3364	8435	843*
3371	—	382
3607	—	87*
3608	—	86
3609	—	85
3685	2335	70*
3687	2325	69*
3688	2320	66*
3689	2310	49
3705	—	35*
3706	—	28*
3708	—	26*
48	9000*	1201*
51	9014	1220
52	9006	1208
53	—	—
57	9002	1203
61	9013T	1218*
62	9000T	1201*
67	—	1211*
69	—	1218*
75	9002	1206*
90	9012T	1217*
91	9008*	1211
92	9011T	1216*
93	9007*	1210*
94	9011*	1216
95	9006T	1208*
99	9005T	1207*
101	9009*	1213*
102	—	1208*
103	—	1210*
104	9012	1217
105	9013*	1218*
106	9002T	1203*
107	9003	1204
108	9014*	1220*
111	—	1218*
112	9003T	1204*
113	9007*	1210*
114	9010	1215
115	9004	1206
121	9007	1210
122	9010T	1215*
123	—	1213*
124	9007T	1210*
125	9009	1213
126	9006*	1208*

SANTA MOTIF

(See color illustration on inside front cover.)

DMC #

	310	Black
⊙	318	Light Steel Gray
⊡	762	Very Light Pearl Gray
⊟	612	Medium Drab Brown
⊠	606	Bright Orange Red
⊞	353	Peach Flesh
\	318	Light Steel Gray (backstitch)
↖	606	Bright Orange Red (backstitch)

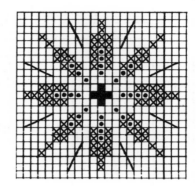

STAR MOTIF

(See color illustration on inside front cover.)

DMC #

	741	Medium Tangerine
⊙	742	Light Tangerine
⊠		Gold Metallic
——		Gold Metallic (backstitch)

CHRISTMAS TREE MOTIF

(See color illustration on inside front cover.)

DMC #

⊠	905	Dark Parrot Green
◥	781	Dark Topaz
⊙		Gold Metallic
——		Gold Metallic (backstitch)

ANGEL MOTIF

(See color illustration on back cover.)

DMC #

⊙	799	Medium Delft
◥	781	Dark Topaz
—	781	Dark Topaz (backstitch)
⊞		Gold Metallic
----		Gold Metallic (backstitch)

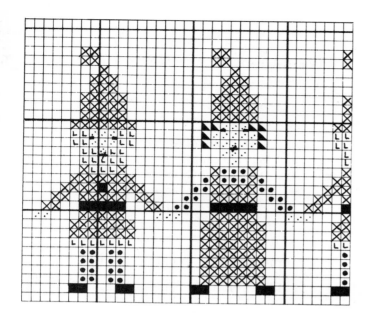

PIXIE MOTIF

(See color illustration on inside front cover.)

DMC #

■	310	Black
⊡	318	Light Steel Gray
L		White
⊠	606	Bright Orange Red
⊡	353	Peach Flesh
◤	780	Very Dark Topaz
—	310	Black (backstitch)
⟋	606	Bright Orange Red (backstitch)

ANGEL & TREE MOTIF

(See color illustration on front cover.)

DMC #

◤	780	Very Dark Topaz
ξ	780	Very Dark Topaz (backstitch)
⊡	444	Dark Lemon
—	444	Dark Lemon (backstitch)
·····	928	Light Gray Blue (backstitch)
⊡	353	Peach Flesh
⊠	905	Dark Parrot Green
L		White
⟋	780	Very Dark Topaz (backstitch)

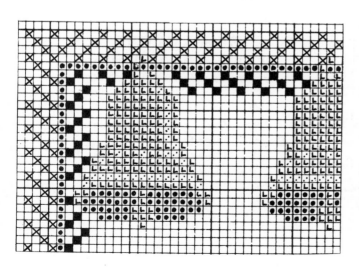

BELL BORDER PLACE MAT

(See color illustration on inside front cover.)

DMC #

⊡	780	Very Dark Topaz
L	972	Deep Canary
⊡	973	Bright Canary
■	3345	Dark Hunter Green
⊠	906	Medium Parrot Green

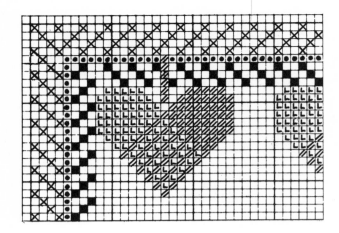

WEAVE-A-HEART PLACE MAT

(See color illustration on inside front cover.)

DMC #

⌶	972	Deep Canary
▨	606	Bright Orange Red
◨	780	Very Dark Topaz
■	3345	Dark Hunter Green
⊠	906	Medium Parrot Green

CANDLE MOTIF

(See color illustration on front cover.)

DMC #

	310	Black
◨	606	Bright Orange Red
⊟	608	Bright Orange
◉	741	Medium Tangerine
⌶	307	Lemon
⊠	907	Light Parrot Green
⊡		White

STAR & CANDLE CHRISTMAS STOCKING

(See color illustration on inside front cover.)

DMC #

—	905	Dark Parrot Green (backstitch)
�	434	Light Brown
⊠	972	Deep Canary
	310	Black
◉	606	Bright Orange Red

EVERGREEN GARLAND

(See color illustration on inside front cover.)

DMC #

◣	904	Very Dark Parrot Green
☒	906	Medium Parrot Green
⊡	606	Bright Orange Red
▥	740	Tangerine
⅂	972	Deep Canary

EVERGREEN HEART

(See color illustration on inside front cover.)

DMC #

☒	731	Dark Olive Green
⊡	606	Bright Orange Red
⬯	905	Dark Parrot Green
		(lazy daisy stitch)

MINI CHRISTMAS STOCKINGS

(See color illustration on inside back cover.)

DMC #

☒	606	Bright Orange Red
⊡	796	Royal Blue
⊿	799	Medium Delft
- - - -	799	Medium Delft (backstitch)
◪	433	Medium Brown
──	433	Medium Brown (backstitch)
⊙	972	Deep Canary
......	972	Deep Canary (backstitch)
┼	987	Dark Forest Green (backstitch)
	310	Black

GOLDEN HEARTS

(See color illustration on inside back cover.)

DMC #

■	3011	Dark Khaki Green
⊡	502	Blue Green
☒	503	Medium Blue Green
⌐	725	Topaz
◣	900	Dark Burnt Orange
◺	947	Burnt Orange

NAPKIN

PLACE MAT

EVERGREEN & SNOWFLAKE SET

(See color illustration on inside front cover.)

DMC #

⊠	702	Kelly Green
——	702	Kelly Green (backstitch)
⊡ ⊙		Gold Metallic
…….		Gold Metallic (backstitch)

HEARTS & CANDLES BELLPULL

(See color illustration on inside front cover.)

DMC #

⊘	606	Bright Orange Red
Ⅴ	743	Medium Yellow
⬭	905	Dark Parrot Green (lazy daisy stitch)
✕	3011	Dark Khaki Green
Ⅱ	310	Black

ANGEL & TREE TABLE RUNNER

(See color illustration on inside front cover.)

DMC #

C		White
—		White (backstitch)
⊥		White (straight stitch; use additional strands)
⊠	434	Light Brown
⊡	353	Peach Flesh
⊘		Gold Metallic

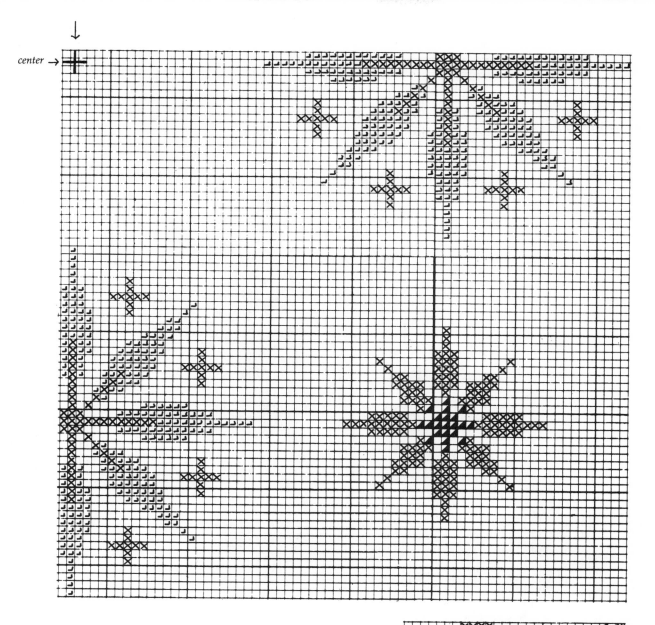

GOLDEN STARS

(See color illustration on inside front cover.)

DMC #

◢ 976   Medium Golden Brown
⊠ 977   Light Golden Brown
◰ 725   Topaz

BORDER

**ELF & HEART
TABLECLOTH**

ELF & HEART TABLECLOTH

(See color illustration on inside back cover.)

DMC #

⧄	817	Dark Coral Red
△	350	Medium Coral
⌣	350	Medium Coral (backstitch)
L	972	Deep Canary
◣	806	Dark Peacock Blue
Ⅲ	807	Peacock Blue
N	993	Light Aquamarine
●	801	Dark Coffee Brown
—	801	Dark Coffee Brown
		(backstitch)
S	552	Dark Violet
⧄	554	Light Violet
⊞	701	Light Christmas Green
O	352	Light Coral
Ⅱ	353	Peach

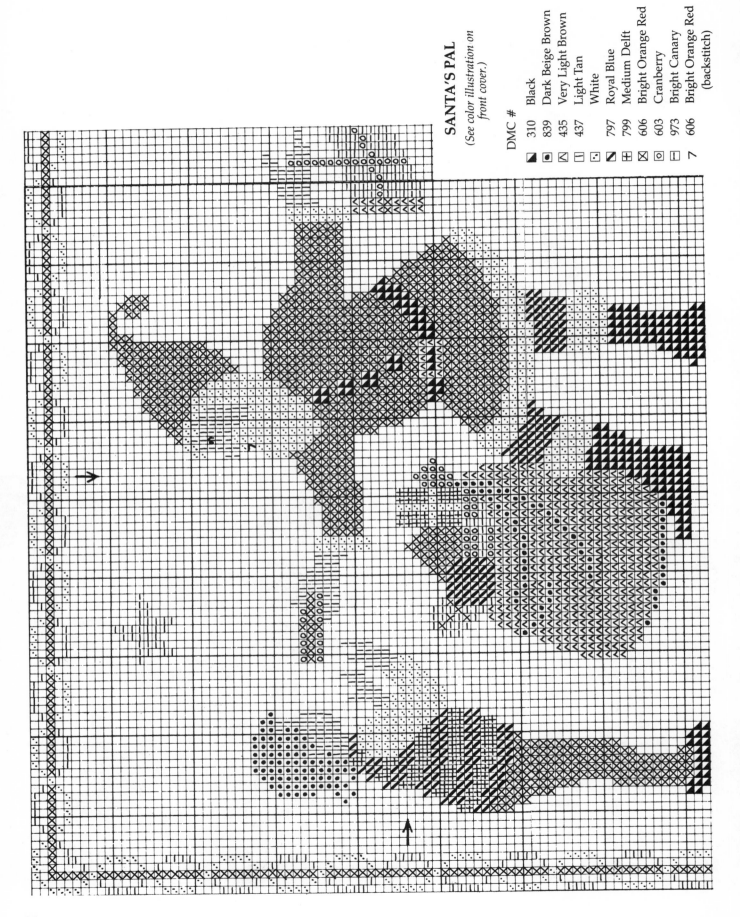

SANTA'S PAL

(See color illustration on front cover.)

DMC #

◪	310	Black
◕	839	Dark Beige Brown
◹	435	Very Light Brown
▯	437	Light Tan
⬚		White
◪	797	Royal Blue
⊞	799	Medium Delft
⊠	606	Bright Orange Red
⊙	603	Cranberry
▯	973	Bright Canary
7	606	Bright Orange Red (backstitch)

HOLIDAY BASKET

(See color illustration on inside front cover.)

	DMC #	
⬛	606	Bright Orange Red
▶	304	Medium Christmas Red
◩	762	Very Light Pearl Gray
◪	415	Pearl Gray
◪	414	Dark Steel Gray
⊡	726	Light Topaz
C	225	Very Light Shell Pink
◩	224	Light Shell Pink
◕	223	Medium Shell Pink
◤	310	Black
⊡	922	Light Copper
⊠	921	Copper

	DMC #	
▽	680	Dark Old Gold
③	869	Very Dark Hazel Nut Brown
◤	610	Very Dark Drab Brown
◥	729	Medium Old Gold
⊡	676	Light Old Gold
◪	989	Forest Green
⊘	987	Dark Forest Green
●	895	Dark Christmas Green
□	471	Very Light Avocado Green
◪	470	Light Avocado Green
◪	3012	Medium Khaki Green

EVERGREEN CANDLE

(See color illustration on back cover.)

	DMC #	
◤	780	Very Dark Topaz
●	905	Dark Parrot Green
⊠	906	Medium Parrot Green
L	907	Light Parrot Green
◼	310	Black
◤	321	Christmas Red
◪	606	Bright Orange Red
C	352	Light Coral
⊞	741	Medium Tangerine
⊡	444	Dark Lemon

ANGEL WREATH

(See color illustration on inside back cover.)

DMC #

⊙	608	Bright Orange
⊡	353	Peach Flesh
◣	781	Dark Topaz
⊠	747	Very Light Sky Blue
⊔		Gold Metallic
──		Gold Metallic
		(backstitch)

HEART WREATH

(See color illustration on inside back cover.)

DMC #

◙	3051	Dark Gray Green
◪	701	Light Christmas Green
▷	703	Chartreuse
◹	972	Deep Canary
⊠	606	Bright Orange Red
◹	608	Bright Orange

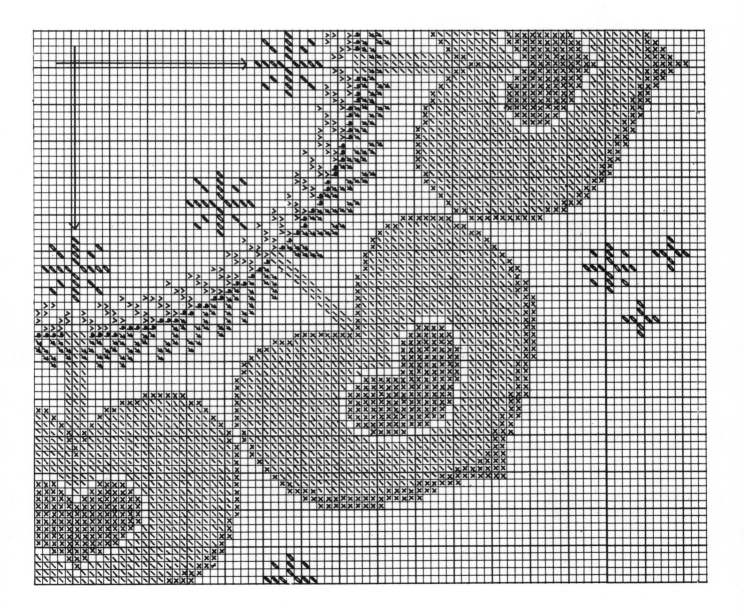

ROBIN-IN-THE-HOLLY

(See color illustration on inside back cover.)

	DMC #			DMC #	
◥	3345	Dark Hunter Green	■	310	Black
⊟	3346	Hunter Green	⬚	414	Dark Steel Gray
◬	470	Light Avocado Green	◥	3024	Very Light Brown Gray
⊞	472	Ultra Light Avocado Green	⊙	921	Copper
◣	838	Very Dark Beige Brown	⊞	922	Light Copper
◪	610	Very Dark Drab Brown	◎	349	Dark Coral
⫼	611	Dark Drab Brown			

RINGING BELLS GARLAND

(See color illustration on inside front cover.)

DMC #

◥	782	Medium Topaz
◿	725	Topaz
⊡	745	Light Pale Yellow
◉	606	Bright Orange Red
◺	608	Bright Orange
⊙	741	Medium Tangerine
⊠	988	Medium Forest Green

SNOWMAN

(See color illustration on inside back cover.)

DMC #		
☑	826	Medium Blue
☑	813	Light Blue
☑	828	Ultra Very Light Blue
③	972	Deep Canary
☑	307	Lemon
☒	608	Bright Orange

DMC #		
—	608	Bright Orange (backstitch)
☑	310	Black
☑	318	Light Steel Gray
☑	906	Medium Parrot Green
☑		White
– – –		White (backstitch)

26

SNOW WOMAN

(See color illustration on back cover.)

DMC #			DMC #	
C	307	Lemon	816	Garnet
	725	Topaz	310	Black
	740	Tangerine	704	Bright Chartreuse
	355	Deep Terra Cotta	702	Kelly Green
	603	Cranberry	828	Ultra Very Light Blue
	601	Dark Cranberry		White

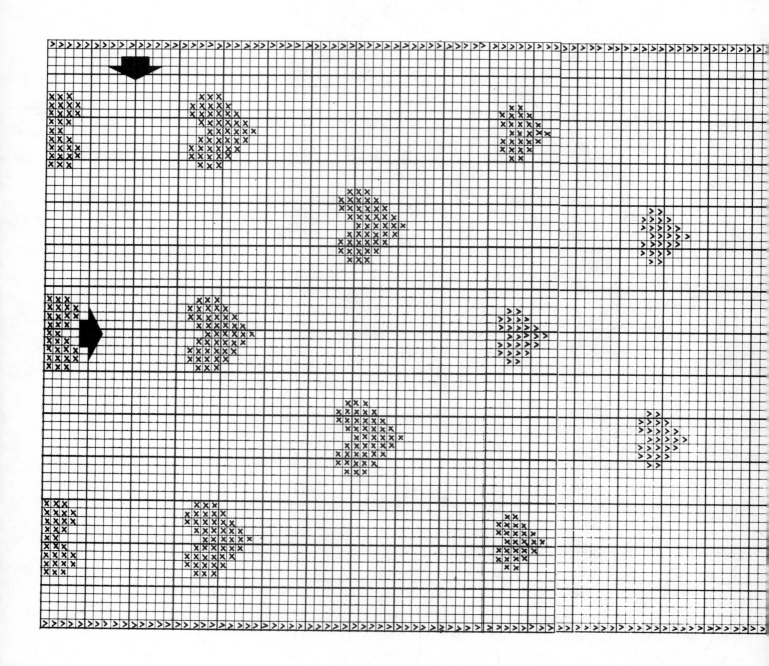

PIXIE TABLE RUNNER

(See color illustration on inside back cover.)

DMC #

☑	608	Bright Orange
☒	817	Very Dark Coral Red
⊟	807	Peacock Blue
➔	797	Royal Blue
◖	310	Black
—	310	Black (backstitch)
⊡	973	Bright Canary
◪	352	Light Coral
◩	353	Peach Flesh
❯	608	Bright Orange (backstitch)

ANGELS & FLOWERS
TABLE RUNNER

(See color illustration on inside back cover.)

DMC #

⊞	518	Light Wedgwood
⊠	519	Sky Blue
■	988	Medium Forest Green
.....	988	Medium Forest Green (backstitch)
◥	781	Dark Topaz
⊙	350	Medium Coral
⊟	894	Very Light Carnation
	310	Black
⊡	758	Light Terra Cotta
----	758	Light Terra Cotta (backstitch)
⊡	353	Peach Flesh
⊡		Gold Metallic
———		Gold Metallic (backstitch)
⟨	350	Medium Coral (backstitch)

Work stems in skirts in Medium Forest Green (backstitch).

TRIMMING THE TREE

(See color illustration on inside back cover.)

DMC #

■	310	Black
⦿	817	Very Dark Coral Red
⊠	350	Medium Coral
⊙	761	Light Salmon
⊡	353	Peach Flesh
◨	433	Medium Brown
⊡	726	Light Topaz
⊠	798	Dark Delft
◪	799	Medium Delft
◩	730	Very Pink Olive Green
⊟	988	Medium Forest Green
⌊	415	Pearl Gray
	783	Christmas Gold
—	783	Christmas Gold (backstitch)
✚✚	350	Medium Coral (backstitch)
---	433	Medium Brown (backstitch)

34

ANGEL CHRISTMAS STOCKING

(See color illustration on inside back cover.)

DMC #

■	3345	Dark Hunter Green
⊠	906	Medium Parrot Green
⊡	761	Light Salmon
·	754	Light Peach Flesh
◉	780	Very Dark Topaz
▨	972	Deep Canary
⊠	800	Pale Delft
∟		White
—	972	Deep Canary (backstitch)

36

STARRY NIGHT

(See color illustration on inside back cover.)

DMC #

◨		White
◼	310	Black
◨	796	Dark Royal Blue
L	827	Very Light Blue
●	550	Very Dark Violet
S	815	Medium Garnet
∧	608	Bright Orange
⊞	3064	Spice
○	972	Deep Canary
⋯	972	Deep Canary (backstitch)
—	310	Black (backstitch)

CHRISTMAS TREE

(See color illustration on back cover.)

DMC #

⊞	905	Dark Parrot Green
◢	606	Bright Orange Red
⊙	972	Deep Canary
	310	Black
◬	813	Light Blue
◩	553	Medium Violet
●		Gold Metallic
◪		Silver Metallic

CHRISTMAS OUTING
ADVENT CALENDAR

(See color illustration on back cover.)

DMC #

⊡	666	Bright Christmas Red
⊠	608	Bright Orange
⟁	742	Light Tangerine
⊞	444	Dark Lemon
⊙	352	Light Coral
⊡	353	Peach Flesh
⫿	702	Kelly Green
⊠	907	Light Parrot Green
⫿	518	Light Wedgwood
⊟	519	Sky Blue
■	646	Dark Beaver Gray
S	648	Light Beaver Gray
----	648	Light Beaver Gray (backstitch)
◣	434	Light Brown
——	434	Light Brown (backstitch)
⧄	3045	Dark Yellow Beige
⌇	3045	Dark Yellow Beige (backstitch)
⊡		White
⋁	608	Bright Orange (backstitch)

BORDER

444

444

DELIVERING GIFTS
ADVENT CALENDAR

(See color illustration on back cover.)

DMC

■	310	Black
⊟	645	Very Dark Beaver Gray
⊞	647	Medium Beaver Gray
◣	3011	Dark Khaki Green
◿	905	Dark Parrot Green
▨	906	Medium Parrot Green
S	798	Dark Delft
⊓	799	Medium Delft
◪	434	Light Brown
⊟	680	Dark Old Gold
◺	729	Medium Old Gold
◉	606	Bright Orange Red
⊠	608	Bright Orange
L	742	Light Tangerine
N	208	Very Dark Lavender
⊙	352	Light Coral
⊡	353	Peach Flesh
......	647	Medium Beaver Gray (backstitch)
∿∿∿	742	Light Tangerine (backstitch)
⊬⊬⊬	434	Light Brown (backstitch)
⌄	608	Bright Orange (backstitch)

BORDER

44

BORDER

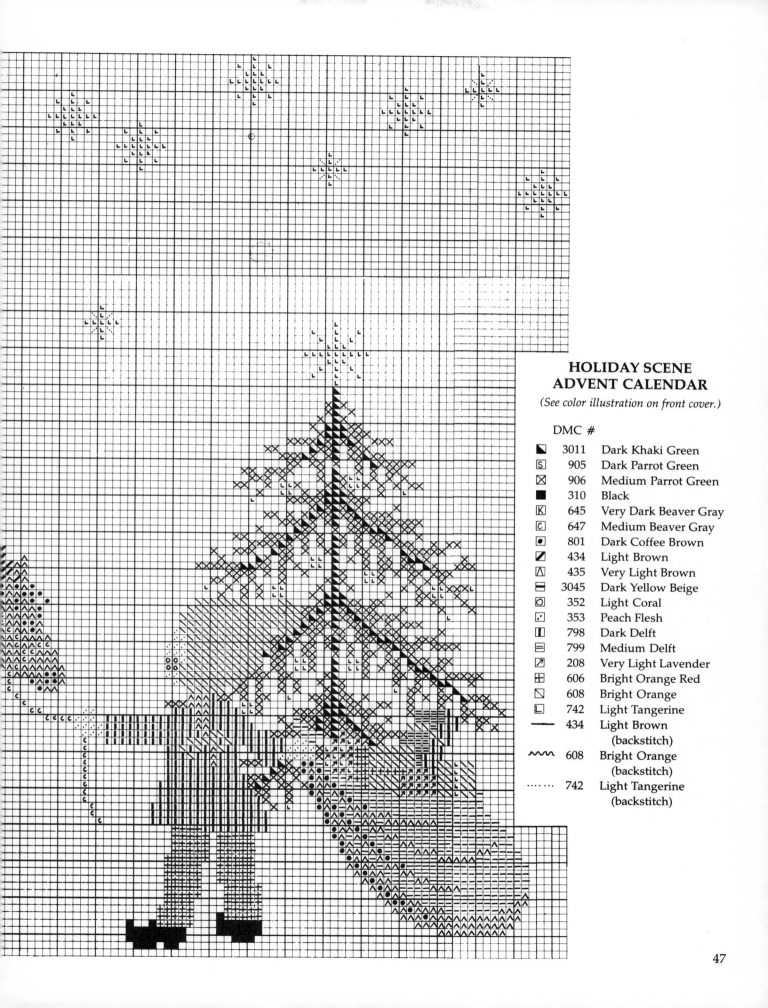

HOLIDAY SCENE
ADVENT CALENDAR

(See color illustration on front cover.)

	DMC #	
◣	3011	Dark Khaki Green
S	905	Dark Parrot Green
⊠	906	Medium Parrot Green
■	310	Black
K	645	Very Dark Beaver Gray
C	647	Medium Beaver Gray
⊙	801	Dark Coffee Brown
∕	434	Light Brown
∧	435	Very Light Brown
⊟	3045	Dark Yellow Beige
◖	352	Light Coral
⋰	353	Peach Flesh
�II	798	Dark Delft
⊟	799	Medium Delft
⊿	208	Very Light Lavender
⊞	606	Bright Orange Red
◺	608	Bright Orange
L	742	Light Tangerine
—	434	Light Brown (backstitch)
∿∿∿	608	Bright Orange (backstitch)
⋯⋯	742	Light Tangerine (backstitch)

EVERGREEN & HEART TABLE RUNNER

(See color illustration on inside back cover.)

DMC #

◿	906	Medium Parrot Green
◩	905	Dark Parrot Green
◪	986	Very Dark Forest Green
◨	732	Olive Green
⊡	606	Bright Orange Red
◪	947	Burnt Orange
——	947	Burnt Orange (backstitch)